ABOUT WAYNE DYER

Wayne Dyer h̶ ... e
'Father of M ...
the field of sel ...
An award-winn ... to the
International Spe ... and awarded
the prestigious Ge ... ward from Toast-
masters Internation ... is the author of 14 books,
which have sold over 48 million copies worldwide.

ABOUT LEON NACSON

Leon Nacson was born in Alexandria, Egypt, to
Greek parents. He is a well-established Australian
book publisher and the founder of the *Planet*
newspaper, a publication that deals with the
environment, healthy lifestyles and personal
development issues. He has also facilitated seminars
and workshops for such notable teachers as Louise
L. Hay, Wayne Dyer, Denise Linn, Shakti Gawain,
Deepak Chopra and Stuart Wilde.

BOOKS BY WAYNE DYER

Everyday Wisdom
No More Holiday Blues
Pulling Your Own Strings
The Sky's The Limit
You'll See It When You Believe It
Gifts from Eykis
101 Ways To Transform Your Life
Real Magic
Staying on the Path
What Do You Really Want For Your Children
Your Erroneous Zones
Your Sacred Self
Manifest Your Destiny
A Promise Is A Promise

BOOKS BY LEON NACSON

A Dreamer's Guide to the Galaxy
I Must Be Dreaming
Cards, Stars and Dreams
(co-authored by Matthew Favaloro)
Deepak Chopra's World of Infinite Possibilities
Stuart Wilde's Simply Wilde
Aromatherapy for Lovers & Dreamers
(co-authored by Karen Downes and Judith White)
Aromatherapy for Meditation & Contemplation
(co-authored by Karen Downes and Judith White)

WAYNE
DYER

How to Manifest Your Heart's Desires

LEON NACSON

RIDER

LONDON · SYDNEY · AUCKLAND · JOHANNESBURG

1 3 5 7 9 10 8 6 4 2

Copyright © 1996 Wayne Dyer and Leon Nacson (questions and concepts)

First published by Nacson and Sons Pty Ltd., Australia, 1996, under the title *Dyer Straight*.
This edition published in 1998 by Rider,
an imprint of Ebury Press
Random House, 20 Vauxhall Bridge Road, London SW1V 2SA
www.randomhouse.co.uk

Random House Australia (Pty) Limited
20 Alfred Street, Milsons Point, Sydney,
New South Wales 2061, Australia

Random House New Zealand Limited
18 Poland Road, Glenfield,
Auckland 10, New Zealand

Random House South Africa (Pty) Limited
Endulini, 5A Jubilee Road,
Parktown 2193, South Africa

Random House UK Limited Reg. No. 954009

Papers used by Rider are natual, recyclable products made from wood grown in sustainable forests

Printed by Mackays of Chatham plc, Chatham, Kent

A CIP catalogue record for this book
is available from the British Library

ISBN 0-7126-7006-8

Dedication
To Eli, Rhett, Joanne, Shane, Stephanie, Skye, Sommer, Serena, Sands, Saje and Tracy.

Acknowledgements
We would both like to thank Rachel Eldred, Claudia Blaxell, Ronika Joukhador, Leigh Robshaw and Shanna Provost for the many hours of research, editing and proofing.

CONTENTS

Consider the possibility of totally eradicating your personal history from your consciousness, and simply living in the present moment. You will find a new freedom as you realise that you aren't relying on the way things used to be to define your life today.

INTRODUCTION

I'll never forget the first time I met Wayne Dyer. I was having breakfast with our friend and author, Stuart Wilde, when Wayne approached our table. He was covered in sweat and dressed in a T-shirt and loose trousers. He had just completed a five kilometre run. Jogging, he explained, is his daily discipline no matter where in the world he finds himself.

Wayne Dyer is one of the most brilliant thinkers of our time, an inspiring teacher who has helped millions move to new levels of self-awareness and beyond the constraints of the physical world. His genius lies in his ability to empathise with our challenges and awaken the infinite spirit within all of us.

A psychotherapist, Dr Dyer received his doctorate in psychology from the University of

Release the idea that a failed relationship makes you a failure. There are no failed relationships. Every person who enters and exits your life does so in a mutual sharing of life's Divine lessons.

Michigan, and has taught at many levels of education, from high school through to graduate study. He has sold over 48 million books around the world and is also the author of numerous articles for professional journals.

Wayne is quietly intense about his beliefs, but his style is buoyant, humorous and unselfconscious. He has managed to combine a fantastic career as well as eight children and a great family life.

We warmed to one another instantly. He laughed when I told him that when his first book, *Your Erroneous Zones*, hit my desk for review, I immediately put it in the pile of books on sex. I told him how disappointed I had been when I took it home, looking forward to an erotic and sensual weekend of reading, only to discover that the book was about self-empowerment and dealing with emotions!

Wayne and I developed a close relationship over the next five years and I am now his representative in Australia and Asia. During the many Wayne Dyer tours that I have facilitated, hundreds of people have passed on cards and letters asking Wayne for help and advice. After Wayne scribbled out the answers to their questions, we discovered that many had similar themes and decided that the resulting dialogue would make a great book.

I hope what we've put together will serve as a reference tool. There may be thoughts in this book you've heard or read somewhere before, but we decided to leave it all in, because it may help you to

Develop the sense that anything that is destructive to one human is destructive to all. Know that the essence of life force that flows through you flows through everyone. That awareness will give you a loving energy that will help to bring all of us together.

reconfirm or rediscover concepts important to your journey. It's like watching a good movie again – you pick up so much more the second or third time round.

Wayne Dyer speaks with wisdom, and he has an innate ability to lift a person's thinking with a few short words. I trust that you will find encouragement in these pages and be uplifted by Wayne's insights and understanding.

Returning from a seminar late one night, I asked Wayne why he travels so many thousands of miles to speak to auditoriums full of strangers. He turned to me and said with conviction, 'My purpose is to get people to look at themselves and begin to shift their concepts. Remember, we are not our country, our race or religion. We are eternal spirits. Seeing ourselves as spiritual beings without labels is a way to transform the world and reach a sacred place for all of humanity.'

I remember watching Wayne complete a meditation back stage. As he walked through the curtains onto the stage to resounding applause, I sat down in the seat he had just vacated. I could hear him speaking.

'I am talking here today about a higher state of awareness. About reaching what Carlos Castenada talked about as the level of impeccability – the highest level of awareness. About the fact that each and every one of us can make our lives the miracles we would like them to be. We need to understand that we have within us something that is much more divine and much more powerful than we've been led

Entertain the thought that you remove habits from your life by coaxing them downstairs one step at a time. Try to catch individual toxic thoughts in the moment they are occurring, one moment at a time, and you will be able to achieve the transition from toxic to pure.

to believe by all the well-meaning sponsors that have shown up in our lives...'

When Wayne came off stage I asked him why so many people feel dehydrated when it comes to their thirst for spiritual awareness.

'You know, Leon,' he said, 'there are different levels of awareness available to us, but most of us buy into what I think of as the survival level of awareness. But there's a place we can get to that is much higher than that. There are certain things we have to do in order to be able to realise the words that Jesus spoke in the New Testament when he said through St John, "Even the least among you can do all that I have done and even greater things."

'I take that personally and literally. Each of us has within us divine capacities to be able to manifest and create virtually anything we can conceive of in our life, as long as we stay on purpose. Most of us have bought into a set of beliefs and truths that are not available to us, and when these new truths come and knock on the door, we don't know how to open it, even when we want to. Most of us push on the door until the realisation comes that the doorway to this heightened awareness doesn't push outward – it opens inward.'

I knew exactly what Wayne was talking about. How many people did I know who had described their lives just like that? They had learnt about new ways to be, but felt as if they just couldn't live it day to day. They were pushing against the door and wanting so much to step in. So what is the answer?

'You have to really learn to face a different way,'

Keep a journal. In it, describe what offends you about other people. If you can be objective, you will find that what offends you is really a judgement about how others should be behaving. These judgements are that false idea of yourself, convincing you that the world ought to be as you are, rather than as it is.

said Wayne. 'Most of us have been looking outside of ourselves for something that will resolve the difficulties or struggles, or the things that seem to be missing in our lives, because we've been taught that's the way to do it.'

Something that Wayne said in his seminar came back to me. He was using a metaphor to explain how we search in the wrong places for solutions.

'I'm in my house and I drop my keys. The electricity has suddenly gone out, so it's dark and I can't see. In my wisdom I say, "Only a fool would look around in the dark for his keys". I notice that the street lights are on outside, so I go out there to stand under one to see if I can find the keys I dropped. I search but can't find them. Suddenly, a friend shows up and helps me look for them for another half hour. Then he has an insight.

'"Where did you drop your keys, Wayne?" he asks. "What has that got to do with anything?" I reply. "Well, you might just think about where you dropped them," he says. "Well, I dropped them in the house, but it's dark in the house. I'm not going to look in the dark when I can look in the light for what I want," I answer.

'It's an absurd image, isn't it, but that is exactly what we do when we have a problem in our lives. It is located inside, but we're looking for the solution to it out here. We want someone or something to change in order to be able to achieve this heightened, grand, miraculous state of awareness, yet it is available to each and every one of us!'

Curb your need to be right. If you truly want to work on this area of restraining your ego, then simply respond to what someone has said without offering an argument or a piece of advice. As you practice this technique, your ego will fade, and your relationships will improve.

Questions and Answers

The following pages list the most common questions asked of Wayne Dyer. They're not my questions: they're yours or those of your peers. I was the custodian of your cards and letters for a very short time and, through my close association with Wayne, have been able to obtain answers for you and compile them in this book. You may find one of your questions here. I hope so. I thank each and every one of you who entrusted me with your queries, because without you this book would not exist.

CHAPTER 1   *Higher Self and Ego*

What exactly is the Higher Self?

Sogyal Rinpoche said, 'Two people have been living in you all of your life. One is the ego: garrulous, demanding, hysterical and calculating. The other is your hidden spiritual being, whose still voice of wisdom you have rarely attended to.' That is your Higher Self.

How do you know if you are living from your Higher Self?

When you trust in and live from your Higher Self you are consciously practising being kind rather than right, at all moments, with as many people as possible and in as many places. This is being kind

Be still and know. These four words will help you get past striving and help you to know the bliss of being here now. When you allow yourself to be still, you will understand the futility of constant striving or chasing after more.

not only to others, but to yourself, and being kind not only to people, but to all things. God is everywhere. Nothing can be dead because this intelligence is a part of all things. This intelligence is everywhere and honouring it means living from your Higher Self.

How do we know if our Higher Self is prodding us to do something or whether it's just our ego?

The Higher Self pushes us towards more peace, joy, and bliss in our lives; when we are operating from our Higher Self, we feel less competition and less separation from each other. But we don't really allow this part of ourselves to give us the sustenance, joy, and capacity to manifest miracles.

The ego believes strongly in competitiveness and comparing. It's always working against us. It is insane. Insanity is defined as something that is convincing you you're something you're not. You are that which is eternal, changeless, and disembodied, watching, observing, noticing, with no doubt.

We have attachments to labels we place on ourselves. I think reaching a higher awareness is like a disappearing act. If you want to reach this higher state of awareness, you have to give up your primary identification with any label you might have.

You have to abandon the labels and understand this fundamental truth: we are not human beings

Make an attempt to shift your career objectives from self-absorption to a 'calling'. Use your talents and special interests to fulfil your service with your calling. Your life work will take on a dramatic shift towards abundance, and you will feel that you are 'on purpose'.

having a spiritual experience, but spiritual beings having a human experience. The quality of your human experience has absolutely nothing to do with this form you showed up in; with this garage you have parked your soul in for a while.

What are the benefits of letting go of the ego?

Let go of the ego and you get beyond this whole stage of just surviving! You go to a higher place where you begin to literally manage the co-incidences of your life and create an energy where you attract to you whatever it is you need. You will always be in the right place at the right time.

Sometimes I feel I'm in conflict with an 'angel' and 'devil' inside of me. Can you explain this?

There are two people in every one of us, the first person is called the ego – Earth Guide Only. Your Earth Guide is something you will not find in an X-ray or an autopsy. It's just an idea and it's an idea we all carry around that says, 'Who I am is separate from you; who I am is separate from my environment and all things in it; and who I am is separate from God.' The ego says it is separate from everything therefore 'who I am' is in competition with you because I am separate from you. This means I am in competition with you and believe in finite resources, 'There's only so much in this world,

You cannot have a better past, so abandon that thought right now. You did what you knew how to do, given the circumstances of your life. Instead of indulging in regrets, let your thoughts remain on love, and let your actions stem from that love.

and if I don't get mine, somebody else is going to get it before me, so I've got to go after it and beat you otherwise you are going to get it.' I evaluate myself and my success as a person on the basis of how much I get, how much it's worth, how little you have, what it costs, and what the label is, and all these criteria become the work of the ego. The problem of the ego is that it never gets enough. It always wants more. The mantra of the ego says, 'I must have more.' It never arrives and is always striving. So you find yourself in this state of turmoil and you are constantly looking to have a better this and more of that... more, more, more, becomes a way of life.

The second person in each and every one of us is what I call the Sacred or Higher Self and the Sacred Self doesn't really care if you win or lose, how much more you have than everybody else, how much better you are than anyone else... it only wants one thing – peace. A great teacher of mine said enlightenment means to be immersed in and surrounded by peace at all moments of your life. This sacred part of us only wants us to be at peace – it doesn't want us to have more. So this is the battle that goes on within us – it's the battle between the ego and the Sacred Self.

Is the lower self, the ego, to be subjugated?

When I say lower self, I speak of it as being in the material world, but I know in my heart that we are

If enough of us shied away from conflict and confrontation, just imagine how much war we could eliminate.

all one. I am aware of a oneness, but to talk about it I have to put it into words and this requires divisions. Some day I will be able to sit in silence for seven or eight hours in front of an audience and everyone will have a profound experience, but right now I have to talk and this requires pulling things apart even though I am quite aware that we are all one. Reaching the divine is not about attacking the ego, you simply allow the Higher Self to rule more frequently in your life.

At one of your seminars you talked about Siddhi consciousness. Recently, I sat with a woman who instantly brought a sense of peace to my entire being. Is this Siddhi consciousness?

Maybe. It was said of Buddha, it was said of Jesus, that when they went to a village, just their presence would raise the consciousness of those around them. People who are operating at the level of Siddhi consciousness seem to generate a different kind of energy. Energy very much like the invisible energy that plants send out. If you go to a particular street where there are a lot of elm trees and one of the trees gets Dutch elm disease, it will send out pheromones, literally warning all the rest of the trees to protect themselves – the energy produced can be measured. The same kind of energy is in each and every one of us, but those who reach this level of Siddhi consciousness, seem to be able to send it out and affect the rest of us.

Learn to allow others to work out their difficulties without feeling that you are the only one who can fix things. Your ego is pushing you to intervene, while your higher self wants you to experience peace and harmony. Choose the latter.

Recently I noticed how obstinate I can become in arguments. I'll argue a point to death just to prove that I'm right. Of course, nothing is ever resolved and I feel cheated. Do you have any suggestions?

In every moment of your life you have a choice: a choice to be right, which is the ego always at work saying I want to make somebody else wrong, or to be kind, which is the part of you that says I want to be at peace. The question you have to ask yourself is how good can I become at suspending the ego, this need to be right, this need to be important, this need to be self-absorbed, this need to feel superior, this need to acquire, to polish my trophies and merit badges, and how can I instead pick kind? Kind with everyone, including strangers: waiters and waitresses, flight attendants and baggage handlers, your children, your parents, your husband, your wife, everyone in your life. To what extent are you able to choose to be kind rather than right? It's about taming the ego.

Begin to change the vocabulary you use to describe yourself and your expectations. Instead of saying 'Maybe', use 'Certainly'. When you use words that reflect an absence of doubt, you will conduct your life in the same way.

CHAPTER 2 *God and Spiritual Enlightenment*

Is there a guiding force in our lives?

I see everything that shows up in my life as Divine. Everything and everyone is sent to me by this Divine Organising Intelligence that has many names. I don't care what you call it, whether you want to call it God, or Soul, or Spirit, or Consciousness, or the Universal Tao, or Louise! What we call it is not relevant, but it is a very powerful force in us all.

Can this force help us reach a heightened state of awareness?

The Divine Organising Intelligence can be awakened and put to use, and it doesn't have to be

Avoid exaggerating or changing facts for the purpose of impressing others. Persisting in this practice will just keep you from knowing your higher self, which needs no exaggeration to feel important in the eyes of others.

something you believe in. Most of us know about God, but I'm talking about something radically different than knowing about it: I'm talking about knowing it.

How can I come to know God?

Stop needing to be right and practise this as frequently and as often as you can until it becomes your natural response. See if we can work on being kind rather than right. When you find yourself having a disagreement, instead of looking for the part of us that has to be right, stop and say, 'Where do we have agreement and let's discuss that.' Let's see the unfolding of God in each other and in every one we meet.

How do you know if you're on the road to enlightenment?

A sign is when you can start to witness your actions rather than being actively involved in them, and this necessitates being independent of the good opinion of other people, which means you will have to transcend your idea of 'separateness' and tame the ego. The taming of the ego is probably the hardest job you'll ever undertake. Your ability to be the witness, knowing that you are not that which suffers, is a necessary step on the road to enlightenment.

Practice generosity. People who give willingly of their possessions and their money are not doing it because they 'have it to give'. They are coming from a special heart space that is attracted to serving and sharing.

When you say we have to find the witness, what exactly are we looking for?

What we are looking for is that part of ourselves that is eternal and never changes. Certainly it's not in the physical or material domain. Everything in this domain is in a constant state of change. It's always shifting – it's all tomorrow's food. What is eternal is that which is spirit. Each and every one of us has somcone inside who is looking out – an observer, a witness. And this observer, this witness, has no boundaries, no form, and it never ages. Do any of you ever look in the mirror and wonder who it is looking back at you? I looked the other day and said, 'There's an old man renting my face.'

What are your thoughts on enlightenment?

In the West we have been taught that the way to enlightenment is through struggling, setting goals, trying to find our way, falling down, picking ourselves up, setting more goals, falling down again, setting goals again... always thinking about where we want to be. Finally, we reach enlightenment five minutes before we die. It's sort of a depressing picture of enlightenment. It's a philosophy of striving but never arriving. You're always trying to get some place else. Like the purpose of eating a banana is to get to the other end. When you go dancing with someone the purpose of the dance is not to dance but to end up over there. But

*Attempt to remove all enemies
from your thoughts. The same
intelligence that flows through
you, flows through all human
beings. When you know that you
are connected to all, you cannot
fathom striking out at others, let
alone feeling hatred for them.*

enlightenment is really like listening to music in an orchestra; the purpose of the music is not to get to the end but to enjoy every note of it. If the purpose of being in a concert was just getting to the end, then the greatest musicians in the world would be the ones who conducted the fastest.

How long does it take to become enlightened?

Most of us in the West have come to believe that to be enlightened, to be successful, we have to follow a prescribed set of rules and dogma. People believe they need to set goals, struggle, sacrifice, get proper training, find someone who knows more than they do, do an apprenticeship and ultimately reach this place called enlightenment or success, whatever you want to call it. Of course, it's quite OK to do it this way, but if you read Eastern philosophy and become engrossed in the power of the mind and the power of intelligence, you will see the Eastern masters have discovered another way. The Japanese call it *satori*. This means 'instant awakening' – gaining an understanding of something immediately that can change your life forever. Most of us have experienced *satori*. Think back to those times when you have experienced significant and dramatic changes in your life instantly and walked away knowing your life has changed.

Demonstrate tolerance and love by ignoring what may have transpired in the past. Avoid the inclination to make someone wrong by pointing out the fallacies of their point of view with examples from their past. Let go of the desire to communicate.

What are your thoughts on religion?

I think the truth is the truth until you organise it, then it often becomes a lie. In the organisation of something, very often the organisation itself becomes more important than the truth that supports it and we have to be careful of that. When Gandhi was asked about Heaven he said, 'In Heaven there is no religion.' I speak with great reverence towards religion because I think religion is something that can be an instrument for great peace on this planet, and for understanding something more than our physical awareness. Unfortunately, most of the war and carnage that has taken place in the history of humankind has been done in the name of God and that to me is blasphemous.

Everyone I know who speaks about knowing God, knowing spirit, says it was made possible through meditation. Is meditation necessary to get to the source or God?

I don't know how to get to the source without meditation. Ten to twelve years ago I couldn't imagine myself meditating; today I couldn't imagine my life without it. Once you make this contact through meditation, you have a knowing and that knowing becomes so powerful and empowering that you can never doubt God again.

The meditation I present on the CD *Manifesting*

Lighten your material load, starting today. As you do so, less energy is spent hoarding, insuring, moving, polishing and so on. The less attached you are to your possessions, and the more you are able to share them with others unconditionally, the more peaceful your life will be.

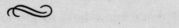

Your Destiny is about an altering of consciousness, and it provides a way to make conscious contact with your source through becoming the person who can no longer be further divided.

If God is omniscient, and his presence is everywhere, then our ego, too, is God. Why then isn't our ego as strong as God?

Think of God as the ocean. I take a glass and I dip it into the ocean and I ask myself what I have. What I have is a glass of God. It's not as big, it's not as strong, it's not omniscient, it's not all powerful, but it is still God. Now I take this glass of God and I pour out one drop and I say to that drop of water, of ocean, of God, 'I want you to sustain and create life. I want you to sustain life and I want to take on the power of the source.' And we watch it and we watch it and it withers away in impotence and dries up, returning to its source. As long as it is separate from its source, it loses the power of its source – that's what the ego has done.

Is Siddhi consciousness the same as Christ consciousness?

In the West Siddhi consciousness is often referred to as Christ consciousness – I sometimes call it transcendent consciousness, too. It is a level of consciousness in which there is no time delay

Allow your higher self to guide you when you have problems. Create a sentence that you repeat silently, such as: 'Please decide for me. I leave it in your hands.' This may seem like a cop-out, but I have found this technique helpful in many problem areas of my life.

between having a thought, any thought, and having that thought materialise on the physical plane. In the New Testament it is referred to as the gift of 'fishing loaves', so when you see hungry people your consciousness is such that you can instantly manifest food, fish, and loaves for them.

If Siddhi consciousness is Christ consciousness, then surely it's not available to all of us?

This level of consciousness is one that, when we hear anyone talk about it, we immediately make the assumption we can't do. We say, 'I certainly can't just think something and have it show up.' Yet if you read the New Testament, St John quotes Jesus as saying, 'Even the least among you can do all that I have done and even greater things.' So the idea that somehow we can't do it is what I think of as the 'conditioning process' we have been raised in and because we believe it, because it goes from a belief to something called a knowing, it becomes our reality and we don't know how to change our agreement with reality to be able to reach this level of Siddhi consciousness. What we can do – and the reason I think we can do it is because if it's in one of us, it's in all of us – is that we can reduce the time lag between our having a thought, having an understanding of the nature of what that thought is like, and having it show up in our physical lives. I'm saying if there's a long time lag or if there's doubt about its materialisation into the physical world,

Know that you are a soul with a body, rather than a body with a soul. Remember that your soul cannot be measured or observed with the tool that you use to view the material world.

then we can eradicate the doubt and we can also attract into our lives what we want – perhaps not instantaneously, but it is possible for each and every one of us. It's something I have been able to do to a much greater extent than I ever thought possible, and it happened when I changed the agreement I had with reality.

*You have a very powerful mind
that can make anything happen
as long as you keep yourself
centred.*

CHAPTER 3   *Inner Self and Heightened Awareness*

How do we make the transition from looking outside for solutions to finding them within?

We have to learn to light an inner candle flame that never flickers, even when the worst hits us. We have to learn to surrender and let go of our attachment to the results and understand that our purpose has nothing to do with the outcome; it has to do with focusing on the process and letting God take care of that process. We don't realise that life is what is happening to us while we're busy making other plans; we're constantly trying to shift our attention outward and be somewhere else.

*When you live on a round planet,
there's no choosing sides.*

How do we gain heightened awareness?

The first step is to erase your past. If you don't have a story, then you don't have to live up to it. Just let go of your story and all of your primary identifications. Begin to erase that part of yourself you used to think of as who you are, and begin to see yourself as something very different than just this physical being that showed up here.

There are four major categories of life: minerals, vegetables, animals and humans. Look at these four things: a rock, a tomato plant, a jaguar and a person. What is it that differentiates them? If you ground them all up, put them together in a bag and sent them off to the lab for a chemical analysis, you wouldn't be able to tell one from the other. Everything on this planet is made up of the same raw material – we are all made of the same stuff!

The Divine Organising Intelligence has taken all the raw material and arranged it into different things, so what separates us from others is not the raw material, but its awareness.

We look at a rock and say it has limited awareness because it just sits there. It doesn't know enough to move out of the rain. A tomato plant has a little more awareness; it produces offspring and moves towards the sunlight, but it's not attached to its offspring. Because we're writing the rules, we say it has less awareness. If tomato plants were writing the rules they'd probably think we were really weird because the tomato plant has babies and says, 'Here, eat my babies. Make marinara sauce out of

*What distinguishes what's alive
from what is dead is growth, be
it in plants or in you.*

my babies; I have no problem with that.' But if you took a jaguar's babies and tried to do the same thing, you'd get a very different reaction.

Then there's us. And the problem with us is that we live our lives at the same level of awareness as animals. We seem content to be in survival mode. We never think of ourselves as having a higher level of awareness that is beyond surviving. We hold onto our beliefs and carry them with us wherever we go.

But if you feel you want to change anything about your life or create something for yourself, you can. If you can conceive it, you can create it – whatever it is. You have the capacity to manifest, but you can't do it the way you've been taught. You really have to get rid of your story.

Seven little words are the key to the universe: 'As you think so shall you be.' Once you know that what you think about expands, you become very careful of what you think about. The corollary of all this is: if you can't conceive of it you can't create it, and that is the problem. We mostly can't conceive of a heightened awareness because we think we are this body we showed up in, and our primary identification is with this thing we carry with us wherever we go.

I believe when you start to let go of your past, you make a divine connection and begin to attract to you that which you need. You think it's just coincidence, but it happens to everybody. Carl Jung called it synchronicity. Everyone has had experiences with synchronicity. It's like a collaboration with fate: you have a thought and what you

Remember that what you think about expands. Since you have the power to make your inner world work for you or against you, use it to create the images of bliss that you want to occur in your material world. Eventually, that inner bliss will be the blueprint that you consult as the architect of your everyday life.

thought of begins to show up. Synchronicity particularly happens when we're not trying to force it to happen. We should let go and allow synchronicity to happen in our lives for us, but instead we say, 'Well it happened before, so I'm going to work even harder at it.' When you work harder, you start to push, and when you start to push, you're starting to tell God how to do it and it doesn't work for you.

Why can't I create miracles in my life?

Your life is the product of the choices you have been making up until now. Think of your life as a ship heading up the river. The ship represents your body. As it's moving ahead you're able to stand at the stern and look down into the water and see its wake. What is the wake? It's the trail left behind by the ship's movement. What is driving the ship? The energy that is being generated by the engine of the ship. Is it possible for the wake to drive the ship? No. The wake cannot drive the ship.

But is this happening in your life? Most of us live the illusion that our wake (our past) is driving the ship; that is, the things that happened to us when we were younger are making us go in our present direction. But it's not true. What is driving the ship of your life is whatever present-moment decisions you are generating in this instant. If you think your past is driving the ship of your life, you cannot get to a heightened level of awareness. In reality, your

Get a clear picture in your mind of something that you would like to see happen in your life: a job opportunity, a new love, quitting an addictive behaviour, or whatever. Keep your inner focus on this picture, and extend love outwardly with this picture in mind. The results will be worth your effort.

past has nothing to do with the way you are today. It's just the trail you've left behind.

We all have this bag of manure we smear all over us and then wonder why our life smells bad. You have to drop the baggage and let go of this insane idea that the wake is driving the ship of your life. You have to understand that the parents you have or had, did what they had to do given the conditions of their lives. You can't ask any more than that. Mark Twain said, 'Forgiveness is the fragrance that the violet sheds on the heel that has crushed it.'

Surrender. Stop the struggle, stop the fight, let go of the goals of where you want to be and where you're headed. Whatever it is you need to know will come to you in meditation if you stay on purpose and allow the inner self to guide you.

It seems that I am perpetually striving for perfection. Am I to be forever disappointed?

Here on the physical plane, everything has a duality. You've never seen a person with a front who doesn't have a back; you've never seen a person with an outside who doesn't have an inside. There's life and death, up and down, left and right, wrong and right, good and bad. Yet there is also that which notices it has no duality. In the Bhagavad Gita it speaks about transcending this paradox, which is probably as close to perfection as you will get.

Be cognisant of the fact that everyone who comes into your life in any capacity is valuable. The petty tyrants are just as divine as those who provided you with encouragement and support. Those whom we judge to be unfortunate or evil can teach us our greatest lessons.

I recognise I am a paradox. Is there any other way?

The great beings who can perform miracles are called non-dual beings and each and every one of us has that within us. We are all non-dual beings. We have to bypass the notion of 'separateness'.

Your mind, your consciousness, your tribal training, and your conditioning, while it is all well intentioned, teaches us to believe we are separate from each other, from the environment, and from God. Because you are 'separate', you have lost the power of your source. This can be debilitating because the power of the source is the ability to create; it's the ability to manifest; it's the ability to heal; it's the ability to be anything we choose. But when we are separate from it we become impotent. So what you are looking to do is reconnect to your source and not separate from it.

Imagine it was light for 24 hours a day, 365 days a year. Would we have a concept called darkness? You wouldn't know such a concept, would you? If somebody started talking about dark, you would have no idea what they where talking about because it was always light. Now think of something that could never know darkness. The sun. Why is it that the sun can never know darkness? Because the sun is the source of all light. In order to be able to transcend this duality you must be able to go to your source. How do I connect to my source? Think of the number that can't be further divided – because to connect to your source means you are no longer divisible. The number of course is 0. You cut

Remind yourself that God created you in perfect love that is changeless and eternal. Your body is changing, as is your mind, so you are not that body or that mind. You were created as a spirit that is pure love. That is where you want to keep your attention focused.

0 in half, it's the same. You multiply 0 by anything you get 0. There is only one 0. There is only one nothingness that we call 0 in mathematics. Now think of something in your experience that is the equivalent of 0. The only thing that cannot be further divided is silence. If you ever ask anyone in India how to seek this source, they will say meditate, meditate, meditate.

Meditation isn't something we do to become quiet and peaceful. Meditation shatters the illusion that we are separate from God, from each other, and from our world. Meditation is the silence you are able to go to, in order to reconnect with your source.

Everyone talks about the importance of trust. Why is trust so important?

When you trust in yourself you are trusting in the wisdom that created you. When you fail to trust in yourself, you don't trust in God. Trusting is knowing. When scientists attempt to put measurements on this thing we call 'divine intelligence' or God, they literally affect it just by needing to observe it. Standards are useless because you constantly have to go back and check what the standard was based upon; you're constantly questioning it. Faith is the only way to know God: a kind of knowing that is independent of anything out there that anyone might try to tell you. It is that kind of trust that is essential.

Spend special moments in awe of the miracle that life truly is. Awe is the loving appreciation of God's work and the presence of the Divine Intelligence.

CHAPTER 4   *Goals and Life Path*

What's the difference between setting a goal or knowing what you want to happen in your life, and pushing against the force?

We don't need to push for it to happen, we only need to have intention. When you have the intention to create something in your life, it begins to show up, which leads us to the second key to higher awareness, which I call banishing the doubt. You can do this really well in your dream state. You have no doubt in your dreams that you can do something. Shakespeare said, 'Our doubts are our traitors.' William Blake said, 'If the sun and moon should ever doubt, they would immediately go out.' The same is true for you.

One third of your life is spent in a dream state. I ask people, 'When you dream, where's the bed?

Instead of cursing the past, bless it and forgive yourself entirely. When you know that all of those experiences were a part of the Divine Design of your life, you can afford to forgive.

What happens to it for eight hours?' The bed is just a symbol of everything you leave behind. If in your dream there are some flowers on the other side of the room and you want to look at them more closely, you just bring them to you. And when you don't want them any more you simply send them away. When you want your grandmother, even though she's been dead for 20 years, there she is. If you need to be 14 again, you're 14 again.

If you need to be married to a jerk for 20 years in your dream, you just say, 'Thank you very much for showing up! I needed an asshole at this point and now you're here.' You don't get mad at the jerk for showing up; you realise you bring to you everything you need for the dream. Then you get to waking consciousness and suddenly you think you're no longer in a dream – and that's the illusion.

Samuel Taylor Coleridge tested our boundaries of belief when he wrote:

> What if you slept, and what if in your
> sleep you dreamed,
> and what if in your dream you went to
> heaven
> and there picked a strange and wonderful
> flower,
> and what if when you woke, you held that
> flower in your hand,
> ah, what then?

The quality of the human experience you are having is dependent not upon the physical form you showed

Be aware of your thoughts, and remind yourself that the simple act of thinking is evidence that there is an invisible energy that flows through you at all times.

up in, but on something much more powerful. There is a place beyond the physical and all is in order, just the way it is supposed to be.

How can we move ideas into our reality?

You can move something from an idea into reality by placing your attention somewhere and refusing to be distracted. When you place your attention somewhere, you are acting out the saying 'as you think, so shall you be'.

The ancestor to every action in your life is nothing more than a reflection of where you have been placing your attention. It has nothing to do with the circumstances of your life. As James Allen pointed out at the beginning of the century, 'Circumstances don't make a man, they reveal him.' The people who are in the worst of circumstances are the ones who need to hear this message the most. If you want to transcend your circumstances you have to challenge the kind of thinking that has brought the circumstances into your life.

How do we erase our past?

If you want to erase your past, you have to believe that those things that happened to you in your life that you don't like are divine.

We have an energy body as well as a physical body. It's an etheric body that's with us at all times.

Try on the concept that beliefs restrict you, while knowings empower you. A belief is merely a mental note attached to your lapel by your mommy. A knowing is etched into the cells of your being, and therefore lives within you with an absence of doubt.

It's like an invisible shield of energy that surrounds us. It determines our perceptions of reality and it is only through being able to shift this energy that we can have clarity and begin to see like we've never seen before. We each have the capacity to shift our energy in terms of our own lives, as well as those around us.

You have the capacity to communicate with anyone on this planet, and communicate with those who have left, because that which is real is that which never changes, and that which was never born, never dies. Each and every one of us is trapped inside something that is constantly changing, but there's a part of us that isn't.

You also have the capacity to heal. It's just a matter of learning how to tune into it. You have to start to rely on your powerful energy body and shift your energy outward. Next you must banish all doubt and open up to the possibility that you are unlimited in the dimension of the formless and in the place in you which has no form.

We're all just physical manifestations of the same essence. That's all we are. When you make your primary identification with that which is watching, that which is the commander, you begin to have a whole new awareness – a knowing. And with that knowing you can project outward and create anything in your life.

Get back to nature. Give yourself time in the woods, trekking in the mountains, walking in open meadow, or walking barefoot on the beach.

I sometimes experience doubt about my ability to create the things I really want in my life. How do I overcome this?

If you experience doubt about anything in your life, that doubt is what you'll act on. What you think about is what expands. Once you know this you start to acknowledge an invisible observer who watches the body go through its motions. You transcend the big lie which suggests there are certain things you can do and things you can't. Everything you know comes from within. Everything you believe is an intellectual act. Everything you know is a metaphysical, cellular act. Shift to knowing. You can't know from instruction: I hear and I forget, I see and I remember, I do and I understand.

The knowing is metaphysical. Once you get it, it stays with you. Knowing will never let you down – beliefs will always let you down. When you have a knowing, don't allow anyone else to smudge it in any way.

To get past doubt you must begin to understand the difference between what it is you believe and what it is you know. Everything you believe was handed to you by someone or something outside of yourself, and therefore it comes attached with doubt. Knowing is a metaphysical experience. In order to have a knowing, you have to rid yourself of all aspects of doubt.

Make a daily effort to look upon others without condemnation. Every judgement takes you away from your goal of peace. Keep in mind that you do not define anyone with your judgement; you only define yourself as someone who needs to judge.

How can we turn challenges into opportunities?

When something negative is happening instead of asking, 'How could this be happening to me?', say to yourself, 'There's probably a real lesson in this. I'm going to detach myself and observe it. I am not my body. I am that which is observing. I know that whatever I'm going through is Divine Order.'

What we have to do is transcend the paradigms we have in life. A paradigm is a way of thinking that we're stuck in. I get up every day at 4a.m. I decided I wanted to challenge a paradigm in my life – the paradigm that I have to have a certain amount of sleep in order for me to have a good day or to have the energy to get through the day. I said to myself, 'Instead of sleeping eight hours a day I'm going to see if I can get it down to four and still have the same energy.'

We sleep at the wrong time. We sleep when we could be talking to God, when it's silent and peaceful and our brain is ready to receive and hear what we need to hear. We're awake at the time when we're most groggy and sleepy. If you spent two or three hours every morning of your life walking in silence along the river, in your backyard – anywhere – your life would change. The ideas that have come to me in these moments have been incredible. And guess what, I don't get tired! If I get a bit sleepy at three in the afternoon, I meditate for ten minutes and I'm fine again.

It's hard for us to get out of paradigms. In 1967 Mother Teresa was asked if she would march

Be conscious of your thoughts, of the make-up of your internal dialogue. Know that any thoughts you repeat that are contrary to your Divine eternal essence are keeping you from experiencing the joyous and complete life you deserve.

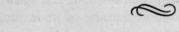

against the Vietnam War. She said, 'No, I will not. But if you have a march for peace, I'll be there.' There's a big difference between being *against* war and being *for* peace. It takes a paradigm shift. What you are for empowers you. What you are against weakens you. So the paradigm shift is to be *for* something.

Instead of looking at what you don't like about someone, think about what you *do* like, and what you think about will expand. When you first meet someone and fall in love you don't say, 'You know, if you were just a bit taller, I'd be crazy about you.'

I feel there is a never ending barrage of blockages standing between me and my goals. How do I overcome these blockages?

One of the biggest challenges we all have to overcome is conditioning. All of us have a set of beliefs and these beliefs were handed to us by what I call the tribe, and when I use the term 'tribe', I don't mean that in any disrespectful way. We have many tribes we show up in: our immediate family, our extended family, our culture, our educational tribes, our religious tribes, our business tribes, our physical/geographic tribes... and all these labels, all of these expectations we place upon ourselves are something that other people have put on to us, and told us this is who you are and this is what defines you and this is what you are responsible for. The members of the tribe, including your parents and

Develop the ability to witness your thoughts by stepping back and watching them enter and exit your mind. Just observing the flow of thoughts will slow the mind down to the still point where you can experience God.

grandparents, taught you many things you needed to know and are very important to know. Success is about transcending tribal consciousness, not putting it down, and transcending tribal consciousness means you come to a point in your life where you are no longer required to rely upon what you have been told by others, what testimony others have given you, or what other people's experiences have been in order for you to act or react – you are free.

Within each and every one of us we have the capacity to attract into our lives what it is we would like to be able to attract; we are able to put our attention on something and have it show up in our lives. The problem is most of us are conditioned to believe that we are limited and this is not available or possible. Challenge the conditioning you have been exposed to in your life, and begin to see yourself as a miracle worker. It's what I call doing a somersault into the unimaginable.

I believe it is possible to create anything you want in life. The problem is I'm not quite sure how to go about it. How do you make it work for you?

It comes down to what you really, really want. The first step really stands for I wish. If you know you have the power to manifest something in your life you perceive to be missing – money, promotion, relationship, removal of an addiction, losing weight, new job – you have to wish it first. A wish is

Become aware that there are no accidents in our intelligent universe. Realise that everything that shows up in your life has something to teach you. Appreciate everyone and everything in your life.

simply an exclamation which says I would like to have this.

The second step really says I desire. The difference between a wish and a desire is that with a desire you are willing to ask for it. You are asking the divine presence if in fact you can have this wish. 'Ask and you shall receive.'

The third step really stands for I will create. Now you have shifted from a desire to a will. *I will have it* is an intention that says, 'I'm going to create this in my life'. So you've gone from a wish to a desire to an intention. Once you have an intention you can only act on what it is you are thinking about.

The fourth step really stands for hardening of the intention, or placing passion/emotion on this thing you would like to attract into your life. When you get a will that is so hardened with so much passion, you can only act on that will. I'm telling you right now that everyone you know who is good at attracting things into their life, whom you call lucky, has the characteristic of having a passionate will that no one else can mirror.

So what you really, really want means, I wish, I desire, I'm asking, I am passionate about attracting it.

I told my friend the other day about my goal to own a home by the time I was 35. She then went on to tell me it was impossible. What do you do when friends or family don't support your goals?

It doesn't make any difference what anybody else in

Anything that keeps you from growing is never worth defending.

the tribe has ever said about your ability to attract what you want into your life, you are going to do it anyway. One of the things I say over and over again about manifesting your destiny is don't share it with anyone. Whatever it is you would like to attract into your life, don't share it with your closest friends, your allies, your soulmates, whoever. The moment you do, you involve the ego, and manifesting does not take place from the ego. Be passionate about what you want to create in your life and go for it, but don't tell others. If you involve the ego, you have to explain yourself, you have to argue for your goal, your dream. You also have to listen to the reasons other people tell you it can't happen, or even listen to the reasons why they think it can. The minute you get the ego involved you stop the manifestation process.

If you think the solution is outside of yourself, but the problem is inside of yourself, then you're living an illusion. The fact is that every problem is in your mind, and so is every solution.

CHAPTER 5   *Our Physical Body and Emotions*

Is there more to us than this physical body?

Yes. There's a divine, formless, unbounded intelligence that flows through you and watches you do the things you do. I know strange and wonderful things have happened to my form since I showed up here. But it doesn't bother me; I become the observer. The person who is doing the watching is ageless, timeless, and formless. You can't see it or get hold of it, yet it is controlling everything.

I seem to get so caught up in my emotions. How can I stop this?

You have to cultivate your witness. This is where

Know that there is an invisible intelligence in everything. You have the power to make contact with this Divine Intelligence and create a life of bliss.

you begin to see that you are much more than your troubles. You are the witness, the observer. Your lower self is abandoned when you cultivate your witness. You can witness your body and your thoughts. You can watch yourself be angry in one moment and blissful in the next. You have to let go of your primary identification with this body and become the witness. As you get good at it you will begin to place your attention only on that which you want to manifest.

I know you can go from poverty, from an alcoholic background, from hunger, or from having no parents around, to a life of abundance, prosperity and fulfilment. I know it. Not because I've read about it or because someone else has told me about it, but because that has been my past. The same thing is true of your experience with God. You can know God by being quiet, being silent, by cultivating the witness, banishing the doubt and, finally, by taming the ego. The ego is that part of you which is attached to being separate and doesn't allow you to think of yourself as connected to all.

Everyone is on their own path and doing exactly what they are supposed to be doing. There are no accidents. For example, you may be with someone who is not only not on your path, but not even on an entrance ramp to your path. But you signed up for it! If you don't want them in your life ask yourself, 'Why did I attract him/her?', instead of, 'Why does he/she keep showing up?'

Forgiveness is the most powerful thing you can do to get on the spiritual path. If you can't do it, you can forget about getting to higher levels of awareness and creating real magic in your life.

I've had a problem with my weight for years. Over the past few months I have been trying to focus on becoming my perfect weight. I'm dieting, exercising, affirming... nothing seems to work. I'm sure I'm going to be obese for the rest of my life. Is there anything more I can do?

You can't attract thin into your life from a consciousness that says I dislike being fat, just as you can't attract into your life prosperity from a consciousness that says I dislike being poor, because what you really, really, really, really don't want you will get. If what you think about is what expands, and what you're thinking about is what you don't want, then what you don't want will expand into your life. So if your thoughts are on 'I dislike' then what it is you dislike will continue to show up in your life. If you think, 'I dislike being overweight', then being overweight will be what you manifest.

If I was to give you one million dollars and say, 'Here, take this one million dollars, go to the shopping mall and buy anything you want', you would say, 'Wow, that's great.' Suppose you get to the mall and the first store you look at sells oriental rugs. You buy an oriental rug that you dislike and throughout your entire shopping spree, every time you come across something you don't like, you take the currency you have for attracting what you do want and use it to attract what you don't want. This is crazy, yet it is exactly what we do when we put our attention on what we don't want and wonder why it keeps showing up in our life.

The whole universal system is held together through love, harmony and cooperation. If you use your thoughts according to these principles you can transcend anything that gets in the way.

The trick is to figure out a way to always keep your passionate intention on what it is you want and never allow what is, has been, what everyone else tells you, to ever show up in your world. This requires being independent of the good opinion of other people.

It seems to me that everyone today has an addiction of some kind. What exactly is addiction?

Most of us are addicts of one kind or another. An addiction can be defined as never getting enough of what you despise. Addiction involves taking something outside of us that we feel we must have for immediate pleasure. We feel this immediate pleasure is freedom but it is really only counterfeit freedom. It's counterfeit because you can never get enough of it and it begins to own you.

I had something to drink every single day for a long period of time. Never drunk, never out of it, but still every day. My teacher said to me very specifically and clearly, 'If you want to be able to play the game at the level I would like to take you to you will have to experience complete sobriety,' and I said, 'I have no trouble with sobriety, I just want a few beers in the evening.' And he said, 'No.'

I stopped after a meditation session where a voice said quite clearly, 'You've tried everything else, now try me.' I was free. In the recovery movement they call it 'Letting Go and Letting God',

If you take two sentences out of your life: 'I'm tired,' and 'I don't feel well,' you will have cured about 50 per cent of your tiredness and your illness.

or not looking for your Higher Self or sacred power in something external to yourself.

Every addiction has three aspects: the craver, the craving, and that which is craved, and they keep you in a constant state of turmoil and toxicity. The craver is you, this body, the craving is the idea I have to have something, that which is craved is whatever it is that is outside yourself you want. As long as you look for it 'out there' you still believe you are separate from it and that separation is what keeps you from peace.

*In order to make a visualisation
a reality in the world of form,
you must be willing to do
whatever it takes to make it
happen.*

Chapter 6   *Personal Growth and Living Your Dreams*

How come when I feel like I'm really achieving growth in my life, something negative comes along and knocks me down?

The Kabbala says not only do you need to have a certain amount of energy to be able to generate a shift in energy, but in order to generate that energy, you must first fall. You must experience a fall in order to move from one level to the next. That's how it works. You go down to get up.

Every fall you have experienced in your life has been nothing more than God saying, 'Here's how I get your attention.' What do you think a divorce, breakup, accident, or illness is about? The ego is very protective about you having a crisis because when you have a crisis you find God, and the ego is

If you build a house that has as its foundation only one support system and that particular support collapses, your entire house will topple.

terrified of God. The ego is terrified of you finding the higher place within, that will transcend virtually anything you call a problem.

When you go there and find that place called God you'll begin to see that every transcendent move in your life was generally preceded by some kind of fall.

When did you first find the strength to move forward?

It was in a moment of prayer years and years ago. I was on my knees and God said to me, 'Wayne, you've tried everything else, now try me.' And it was done. Instant awakening! I turned my higher power into the blessing that it is, instead of relying on the ego.

I want to make the transition, but I keep hearing negatives in my head every time I try to stretch my awareness. How do I stop this?

Shut down the inner dialogue. The inner dialogue is the constant chatter that's always going on in your mind, and it's just a repetition of all the beliefs you've had handed to you by other people.

Your mind is like a pond, and the surface of the pond is where all the disturbances are. If you had a pebble and dropped it, you would see it dropping from chatter through to quiet. Usually it drops

Blame is a neat little device that you can use whenever you don't want to take responsibility for something in your life. Use it and you will avoid all risks and impede your own growth.

beneath the surface, which is what I call analysis. This is the intellectual violence where we pick apart our thoughts. Analysis is anally retentive.

The pebble goes below analysis to synthesis, where instead of seeing how things are torn apart, you see how things are held together. Ultimately, the pebble goes further until it begins to quiet the mind and finally it reaches the place where you empty the mind. The pebble comes to rest in this place which we call 'the unified field of all possibilities'. The poet Rumi wrote:

> Out beyond all ideas of right doing and
> wrong doing, there is a field.
> I'll meet you there.
> You can meet your love there.

I know fear is holding me back from following my dream. What do you suggest I do?

Get rid of conditioning and break free from tribal consciousness. If you are able to do this then, and only then, can you get to the place where dreams become real. As long as you are relying upon what others have told you, or your truth is based upon the experience of others, then what others have told you and their experiences is what you will continue to manifest in your life. Fear usually arises when you walk against the grain of what others have said; work towards forgetting what the tribe has taught you and towards believing that you can achieve

The only difference between someone who's beautiful and unattractive is a judgement. There's nobody in the world who is unattractive. No one on this planet. Unattractive is just what people decide to believe.

anything you place your attention on. There are really only two emotions, fear and love, and love is letting go of fear.

I've been an English teacher for 30 years. During this time I've dreamt of becoming a writer but don't know where to begin. What can I do to get started?

If you want to master something you have to go through the four pathways to mastering. The pathways are similar to the archetypes Carl Jung talked about. He said the four archetypes of adulthood are the athlete, which is the time in our adult life when our emphasis is on our body, what it can do, how beautiful it is, how strong it is. Then we move from the athlete to the warrior, which is the age of the ego, the time when we go out into the world and set goals, think about ourselves and get as much as we possibly can. This is followed by the archetype of the statesmen, the time when we stop thinking about our own quotas and what's in it for me, and we see what's in it for others and how we may serve. Ultimately, you get to the archetype of the spirit which is when you finally recognise we are not really human beings having a spiritual experience, but spiritual beings having a human experience.

The first of the four pathways is the pathway of discipline – the time of the athlete. For example, if you've never hit a tennis ball before and you want to learn how to play tennis, you go out and you hit,

Deficiency-motivated people
spend their lives in the disease
called more – always trying to
acquire something to make
themselves feel complete and to
repair the deficiency.

and you hit, and you hit; you practise, practise, practise... but that's not enough. Then you have what is called the pathway of wisdom, where you apply the intellect to what it is you are doing. So you learn all the different shots, you learn how to slice, you learn how to hit top spin and over heads and serves and backhands, and all aspects of the game. The third pathway is the pathway of unconditional love. Most of us aren't at 'blissed' in our life we're at 'pissed' in our life, and you have to figure out how to go from pissed to blissed. It's important in your life to do what you love and love what you do. You are approaching a stage of enlightenment when you can't tell the difference between work and play. If you are not doing what you love or loving what you do you have two choices: you either change what you do or change how you feel about doing it and fall in love with it. The fourth pathway to mastery is the pathway of surrender. This is where you surrender the little mind to the big mind, where you allow God to work through you. You let go and you let God – you allow. When they asked Picasso how he painted he said, 'When I enter the studio I leave my body at the door, the way the Moslems leave their shoes at the door when they enter the mosque, and I only allow my spirit in there.'

When you let go and have discipline, wisdom, and love for what it is you are doing and just allow, the most phenomenal things begin to show up and take place in your life.

I've disciplined myself, I've done the preparation, I've read, I've studied, I've used the wisdom I

Children need to know that the words 'It's impossible' are not a part of your vocabulary and that you are a supporter of their dreams.

have and I love what I do, and since I've sur-
rendered I can do whatever I've committed myself
to.

*Over the years I've worked on improving my self-
esteem. Friends and family have noticed my efforts
and have often tried to support me by telling me I
am special. Something about the concept of being
'special' doesn't gel with me. What exactly does it
mean to be special?*

When we know God we are talking about the
source of all life: the intelligence that opens flowers,
keeps the galaxy in place, keeps the planet orbiting,
grows our hair, beats our heart, etc, and this
intelligence, this Tao, this God, this soul, this
consciousness, is universal, it is always flowing, it is
inexhaustible, and most importantly it does not
discriminate. The ego tells us we are special, we are
important, and we are separate, and I say we are not
special, because if you are special, someone else is
not – that's what special means: I am 'better than',
and if your ego doesn't like this and says 'all right,
then we are all special', then we don't need a word
like special, do we?

Detachment is the absence of a need to hold on to anyone or anything. It is a way of thinking and being which gives us the freedom to flow with life. Detachment is the only vehicle available to take you from striving to arriving.

Sometimes I think the focus on creating success and abundance in our personal lives is selfish. Aren't we ultimately here to serve the whole of humanity, not just ourselves?

Of course. The point is when you create abundance and prosperity in your life, you also create and bring abundance into everyone else's lives. Your work is sacred and we are all dependent on each other. We stop the flow when we think we are unworthy and sit around and do nothing. It's important to honour your worthiness to receive.

Be a student. Stay open and willing to learn from everyone and anyone. Being a student means you have room for new input.

CHAPTER 7   *Relationships and Love*

Is our ideal mate our soulmate?

I wrote an article called 'Your soulmate is the person you can hardly stand'. People will come to me and say, 'I've finally found my soulmate, it's so wonderful. He thinks exactly like I do; green is his favourite colour, green in my favourite colour; we both love asparagus; we both like to get up early; we read the same books; we go to the same movies; we have the same ideas on almost everything; I go to call him on the fax line and he's calling me on the other line telling me what I was going to tell him. I say, "I'll give you three more weeks in this relationship."' My feeling is that in any relationship in which two people agree on everything, one is unnecessary – you're not looking for a relationship, you're looking for a mirror.

*In regard to addictions, when
you are pursuing poisons, you
can never get enough of what
you don't want. You become
what you think about all day
long and those days eventually
become your lifetime.*

Mother Theresa was such a beautiful woman, so full of love. I too want to be able to share the love in me but something is holding me back. What's the difference between Mother Teresa and I?

One of my teachers said the difference between Jesus, Buddha, Mother Theresa and us isn't that they have unconditional love and we don't, it's that they don't have anything else. I've often used the metaphor of an orange. If you take an orange and squeeze it as hard as you can and ask yourself what will come out, you will of course say, 'orange juice'. If I was to ask, 'Why does orange juice come out?', you would say, 'Because that's what's inside.' But then if I was to say, 'Well what if somebody else squeezed it? What if we used a different instrument? What if the timing was out?', you would look at me as if I were odd, because you know all that is irrelevant. When you squeeze an orange you get out of it what's inside.

You can extend that metaphor to yourself. If someone squeezes you, puts pressure on you, or says something you find offensive, and out of you comes anger and hate, tension or fear, anxiety or stress, it isn't because of who did the squeezing or what they said, and it isn't because of the instrument or timing, it has nothing to do with that, our ego tells us it does but the fact is what came out was what was inside. If we change what is inside we change what comes out.

If you take someone living at the transcendental level of consciousness and put them on a cross,

The winning attitude is one that allows you to think of yourself as a winner all the time while still giving yourself room to grow.

crucify and torture them, out of them comes what is inside: forgiveness and love. It's about taking responsibility for what is inside rather than saying it's because of how this happened, or the way someone said something and so on.

When I'm in close relationships I notice I repeat the same patterns. How can I break them?

It comes down to having the courage to be independent of the good opinion of others. Know that peace and love are what you are about and anyone who brings anything else into your life isn't going to get from you anything other than love, i.e. what's inside. It's the essence of unconditional love.

In order to be able to make this conscious contact, you have to really tackle this most difficult paradigm or rule we have had thrusted upon us. A song written by Jackson Brown called 'For a Dancer' sums it up best: 'Just do the steps that you've been shown by everyone you've ever known until the dance becomes your very own.' That's what most of us are: we're dancers and we're doing the steps we have been shown by everyone we've ever known and the dance has become our very own, i.e. we've adopted this dance. Later in the song he says: 'Into a dancer you have grown from the seeds someone else has thrown. Go on ahead and throw some seeds of your own somewhere between the time you arrive and the time you go home, because in the end there is one dance you will do alone.'

True joy and the exhilarating feeling of being at peace with yourself and the world comes to the person who lets his or her physical world flow from the pleadings of the soul.

Also, I've always said life gives exams and if you don't pass them you will keep doing them until you get it right, and ultimately have the awareness that this is not the choice you want to make. So anything you are carrying around from your past that is poisoning you is something you really want to take a look at.

How can you know when you are experiencing love?

When you are experiencing love in your life you are inspired. The word inspired means in spirit. When you are inspired you don't get hungry, the right people show up, you don't think about not having enough money... everything just seems to work. Unconditional love is literally your ticket to higher consciousness.

I've had a number of intimate relationships yet I can't seem to make them work. I know what I want from a relationship but I just don't know how to go about getting it. Any clues?

There's a line in *A Course of Miracles*: 'Infinite patience produces immediate results.' Infinite patience is another word for knowing. If you know something is going to occur, you're infinitely patient. All the rest you leave up to God. You know what you want from a relationship and you wait.

As you become awakened, you're not ego-defined anymore. You're not defined by what you get and how you get it. You're more defined by 'I can be internally more at peace' and 'How can I help other people do that?'

Then you start observing and the things you thought would never show up, do.

My boyfriend and I have the most terrible rows over the most insignificant things. We both usually end up feeling more alone than ever. Is there anything we can do to avoid these rows?

'I can choose peace rather than this' is a very powerful affirmation when you find yourself in turmoil, when you find yourself struggling, when you find yourself living through something you don't want to live through. In order to be able to choose peace, you have to understand that the way you relate to other people is what interferes with your ability to choose peace.

Instead of reacting with your ego, which is the part of you who wants to make somebody else wrong and yourself right, you shift and you go to the Sacred or Higher Self.

You can't get prune juice from an orange, no matter how hard you squeeze it. You can't give hate if you only have love inside.

CHAPTER 8   *To Know or Believe?*

How does a knowing differ from a belief?

You have a whole lot of beliefs and then you have things that you know. The things you know are those things that speak to a truth within you – you know them because you have made conscious contact with them. For example if you had never ridden a bicycle before, never *seen* a bicycle before, and I started telling you about bicycle riding and I showed you this thing with two wheels, a narrow body, and a tiny seat, you would probably look at the seat and say, 'No way.' You might think to yourself, 'It's not possible to get on that and move about', but then if I showed you pictures of people doing it, you would start to remove some of the doubt and, eventually, if I got on the thing myself and rode it around the room you would say, 'I could

Did you ever notice how difficult it is to argue with someone who is not obsessed with being right?

probably do that.' But you still wouldn't know how to do it, even if you believed you could. You would know how to do it when you got on the thing and made conscious contact with it. So when we look at what we know, we know those things we have made conscious contact with.

I've noticed as I get older that things I thought I knew, I didn't know at all. Can we ever be 100 per cent certain about anything we think we know?

It's common to assume we know something when in actual fact we don't. Things we think are absolute truths but aren't, are often not the result of our conscious experience – they are the result of a belief system we have adopted.

Can we ever really know that God exists?

I think there is a big difference between knowing about God, which is usually a belief system we have handed to us based upon the testimony of others, and knowing God – that is, making conscious contact so you literally have the direct experience of God. When you do, you gain the power of God. You connect to God in a sense that God is not separate from you but is connected to you. It's almost as if you have to know that you and God are not separate.

In 1986 on the 60th birthday of Sai Baba,

Abundance is about looking at life and knowing that we have everything we need for complete happiness, and then being able to celebrate each and every moment of life.

1,100,000 people gathered in a little Indian village to celebrate. A reporter from *Time Magazine* asked Sai Baba point blank if he was God. Sai Baba looked at him and said, 'Yes I am. And so are you. The only difference between you and I is that I know it and you don't.' It's that knowing, that conscious contact where you gain the power of the source, you can never doubt.

The death of my husband recently made me question God's existence. Is it natural to doubt the existence of God?

Doubt is natural when you believe in God but not when you know God. Probably the most quoted line in *A Course in Miracles* is, 'If you knew, that is without doubt, who walked beside you at all times on this path that you have chosen, you could never experience fear or doubt again. If you knew that.' That means a complete banishment of all doubt.

The consciousness of the tribe has taught us to have doubts rather than the knowing that is talked about in the parables of Jesus and the lepers. Jesus didn't approach a leper and say, 'You know we haven't had a lot of success with leprosy here. In fact you've got a 30 per cent chance. Should you follow all these instructions and do what I say, you can probably live for two years with this disease, but it's a 30 per cent chance if you take my blessing.' He didn't say this because it is filled with doubt. It's not a knowing, it's just a belief. Jesus approached these

Rulers can remove our outer places of worship, but the inner place, that invisible corner of freedom that is every present in each of us, can never be legislated.

people and said, 'You are healed', and they were.

All my life I've done things for other people – my mother, my husband, my kids. Now I want to do things for myself but don't know whether others are holding me back. Can I ever be sure?

When you have a powerful knowing, no one else in your immediate world can impact on that. In order to reach this knowing stage, you have to be willing to be what I call a scurvy elephant.

When I was in the third grade I came home from school to the orphanage, and I asked Mrs Scarf, 'What is a scurvy elephant?' and Mrs Scarf said, 'A what?' I said, 'A scurvy elephant.' I had heard my third grade teacher telling the principal that I was a scurvy elephant in her classroom. Mrs Scarf said, 'I don't know, I've never heard of it.' She called the principal, and he said, 'Oh that's Wayne, he gets everything mixed up. She didn't say he was a scurvy elephant in her classroom, she said he was a disturbing element in her classroom.' A scurvy elephant is someone who doesn't do things the same as everyone else. This is perhaps the biggest challenge life presents: every day there's the pull to be like everyone else, but others cannot hold you back when you no longer try to live up to their expectations.

Give up the 'want'. Know in your heart that you do not need one more thing to make yourself complete, and then watch all those external things become less and less significant in your heart.

CHAPTER 9   *General Questions*

One of your teachers was Abraham Maslow who talks about the concept of self-actualisation. What exactly is self-actualisation?

When I met Maslow in 1968, he said the most profound thing self-actualised people share is they are independent of the good opinion of other people. Self-actualised people know how to leave the tribe and they have reached a state of consciousness in which they are living their bliss.

Maslow looked at the greatest achievers in the history of humankind such as Christ, Buddha, St Francis, Madame Curie, St Joan, and the more contemporary. He asked what separates them from the rest of us – what traits do they have, how do they think, how do they behave differently? and he called these common qualities self-actualisation.

*You don't get abused because
there are a lot of abusers out
there. You get abused because
you send out signals that say,
'Abuse me. I'll take that'.*

What else do self-actualised people share?

Maslow said that self-actualisers are also detached from outcome; that is, they do not do what they do in order to have something show up for them, they do it because it is their passion – they let the universe handle the details. Also, these people are not interested in controlling or manipulating other people. After continual insult Buddha was asked why he wasn't reacting. He said: 'If someone offers you a gift and you don't accept the gift, to whom does the gift belong?' In other words, you have offered me the gift of your insults, I haven't accepted your gifts, therefore they belong to you.

Princess Diana's death touched the world. Do you think there is anything we can learn from her untimely death?

There's an intelligence to this entire system. We don't always understand it, yet we have to surrender to it and trust it. We know that every one of us who shows up on this planet in physical form, will also leave. We show up exactly when we are supposed to, and a part of us knows that we will leave on time and that there is a purpose to it all.

I think my purpose for coming here was to teach self-reliance because that is all I have done since I was a little boy. Perhaps Princess Diana came here to teach us that it is an illusion that some of us are better than others. Perhaps the idea of royalty and

We are our form and our formlessness. We are both visible and invisible, and we need to honour our totality, not just what we can see and touch.

the fact that we have elevated others in importance to ourselves, is something that is keeping us from transcending and getting to a higher place. Diana became part of the Royal Family and said, 'We are all the same.' Perhaps the great outpouring of affection for Diana, who abdicated her royalty in favour of the people, is the beginning of the end of the idea that some people are born into a higher place than the rest of us.

You have often written about the late Mother Teresa. How has she touched your life?

I think the most astonishing story I can recall of Mother Teresa occurred about four years ago when she visited Phoenix, Arizona, to dedicate a homeless shelter. When she arrived they gave her a special room – it was the only room in the place that had carpeting, all the rest had cement floors, and she refused to sleep in there. She said, 'Give this to one of the people who don't have a home, I don't have to have carpeting,' and slept on a cot on the cement floor.

She visited the Phoenix radio station, KTER, the next morning, and my friend Pat, who is the morning disc jockey, was to introduce her. He said when she walked in, just her presence changed the consciousness of the people in the room. Mother Teresa was about 4"10 and weighed about 80–85 pounds – a tiny little thing, yet every one in the room felt more peaceful in her presence.

Only a ghost wallows around in his past, explaining himself with descriptors based on a life already lived. You are what you choose today, not what you've chosen before.

Pat said to her, 'Mother Teresa is there anything we can do for you here at the radio station to help your cause?' and she said, 'No, there's really nothing you can do.' When Pat asked her what she did each day, she said, 'What I do is I see Jesus Christ every day in all of his distressing disguises.' And he said, 'Mother Teresa, we have a very large radio station here, we could generate an enormous amount of publicity for your cause,' and she said, 'Pat, I'm not here for publicity. I am here to dedicate the homeless shelter and talk about it to the people of your city.' He then tried to rouse her interest with money. He said, 'Mother Teresa, we could raise an enormous amount of money here for your cause,' and she said, 'Pat, I'm not here to raise money, I'm not really interested in money, I just want to tell the people about the homeless shelter and the streets.' Finally, almost desperate, he said, 'Is there anything I can do for you while you are here?' And she looked at him and said, 'Pat, you seem so serious. There is one thing you can do. Tomorrow, get up at four o'clock in the morning, go out in the streets of Phoenix and find someone who is living there who believes he is alone and convince him he's not. That's what you can do.' I can hardly ever tell that story without getting choked up because it's really the essence of everything I talk about.

To be attached to your physical appearance is to ensure a lifetime of suffering as you watch your form go through the natural motions that began the moment of your conception.

If you had 30 seconds to give me an inside pointer, what would it be?

Probably the most quoted line from all of literature comes from Hamlet: 'To be or not to be.' It's the most quoted line because it has a very profound meaning. Yet, while it is a fundamental question, the next line is just as poignant: 'Whether it is nobler in the minds of men to suffer the slings and arrows of outrageous fortune, or to take arms against a sea of troubles and thus by opposing end them.' In other words, are you going to take outrageous fortune and accept what the tribe has handed you, or are you going step out into the sea of troubles and take up your own reins? That is really the question.

Do you think there's a man in Heaven who looks over and watches us?

There are basically two theories of the universe. The first theory of the universe, or of nature, says the universe is a monarchy and God is the King. We are the subjects of the King and, as his subjects, we are inferior to him and not to be trusted, because essentially we are conceived in sin. God in this model is generally a white male in Heaven, who is 'out there' judging us. He is this invisible person who keeps track of all things. The problem with this theory of nature is, if you subscribe to it, you will always be lost. The reason I say you will always be

If you are still following a career path that you decided upon as a young person, ask yourself this question today: Would I seek out the advice of a teenager for vocational guidance?

lost is if you believe in your heart and come to know you are not trustworthy, you will always doubt your validity as a human being. Even your belief in God is something you will always question because it comes from someone who is not to be trusted.

The second theory of nature says God is not really a person but a presence that is everywhere and in all things. There is no place where God is not. In this model, God is a universal presence, a presence called love.

By concentrating on your breathing, by meditation, and by affirming aloud your intentions, you can re-energise yourself on your life's journey.

CHAPTER 10   *Wayne's World*

Wayne, do you like touring?

I love touring. I wouldn't do it for any other reason. I certainly don't need to. I love speaking and I love writing, and in order to speak you have to travel, unless you want to talk to the same people every night. It just goes with the territory. I speak internationally a lot now. I travel to Europe, Asia, South America and Australia regularly. It's like a worldwide revolution, and I just go where I'm sent.

On average, how many cities would you visit in a year?

Oh, about fifty.

You, a person with a vision, are like a pebble in a stream, moving ever outward to infinity, impacting on all who come into contact with the ripple.

How many children do you have?

We have eight: six daughters and two sons.

What music do you listen to when you relax?

Mozart and Jackson Browne.

When you're at home and you get a chance to cook, what dish are you really proud of?

I don't do much cooking, but my veggie burgers have acquired a certain reputation.

Who do you most admire in your field?

I admire everyone who's out there teaching. I have some dear friends whose work I admire. They include Louise Hay, Deepak Chopra, Stuart Wilde, Marianne Williamson and Dennis Waitley.

If you could invite six people from any time in history to join you in a dinner party, who would they be?

Buddha, Jesus, Gandhi, Hitler, Stalin and Alexander the Great.

We send our kids off to school to major in 'labelling' and think the ones who do it best deserve the highest grades.

Where did the title the 'Father of Motivation' come from?

I'm the father of Shane, Stephanie, Skye, Sommer, Serena, Sands, Saje and Tracy. I might as well be the father of motivation too, as long as there's no paternity suits involved.

What is the secret of a successful marriage?

Not making people wrong. Practising being kind rather than right, and treating the marriage as a spiritual partnership.

Where do you see spirituality in the next millennium?

Spirituality is the trend in our world today. We've had the age of agriculture, the age of industry, the age of technology, and now it is time for the age of spirituality. The concept of spirituality means nothing more than recognising that we're all connected. I think the survival of the planet depends upon an awareness that we are all just cells in the same body called humanity.

What is your favourite metaphysical book?

Probably *A Course in Miracles*.

A heart starts beating in a mother's womb six weeks after conception and life as we observe it is under way. It remains a mystery to all of the greatest minds on the planets.

What is your favourite meditation?

The one that I practise. It's called Japa.

What are you working on now?

A book called *Wisdom of the Ages*. It's 60 essays based on 60 great teachers. They go back as far as Buddha and Pythagorus to contemporary people like Mother Teresa and Martin Luther King. It also includes the poets, artists and philosophers of the Renaissance. I've taken a poem or a saying from each teacher, and written an essay based on what they were telling us.

I'm also recording a tape series with Deepak at the Chopra Centre For Wellbeing. It's called *How To Get What You Really Really Really Really Want*. We combine Eastern and Western principles and teach people how to get beyond judgement and reaction in order to make their dreams come true.

Wayne, if you're the 'Father of Motivation', who's the mother?

Let's leave that one for the next book.

You mustn't attempt to will anything. You need only be willing. Even though the sky will be different in a few hours, its present perfection and completeness is not deficient. You, too, are presently perfect and not deficient because you will be different tomorrow.

Books by Wayne Dyer

Everyday Wisdom
Everyday Wisdom is a spectacular collection of 200 of Wayne's most famous quotations and reflections. This inspirational book enlightens the mind, delights the senses, and nourishes the soul.

No More Holiday Blues
Do you get depressed over the holiday season? For some it entails stress and obligations, and for others it is a lonely time. This book will help you overcome holiday depression, and show you how to make your next holiday a joyful one.

Pulling Your Own Strings
A book for anyone who feels victimised, manipulated or controlled. Wayne provides simple steps on how to chart your own course in life and regain your personal power.

To enter the realm of real magic you will have to suspend all thoughts of limitation and become a spiritual being first, a being who has no limitation in your inner domain where boundaries are non-existent.

The Sky's The Limit
Based on the teachings of Abraham Maslow, this book shows how you can live your bliss once you've mastered the traits of self-actualisation. In this practical and thought-provoking book, Wayne shows how you can reach the highest levels of a higher consciousness.

You'll See It When You Believe It
Wayne stretches beyond self-help to self-realisation in this profound, inspiring book. He explores the way to personal transformation by using thoughts constructively. Using anecdotes and examples, he shows us that believing is seeing.

Gifts from Eykis
This is a story about an exchange encounter between an earthling and a citizen from outer space. Wayne uses the parable format effectively, provoking readers to question many of the attitudes ingrained in our cultures.

101 Ways To Transform Your Life
This book provides 101 reminders and ideas that will transform your thoughts for a more positive and fulfilling existence. Just open the book up at any page and find a daily source of inspiration.

Real Magic
In *Real Magic*, Wayne explains how creating miracles in your life can be a reality. He leads the reader through a journey of self-discovery,

Acting as if you were already what you want to become and knowing that you can become it is the way to remove self-doubt and enter your real-magic kingdom.

examining issues such as spirituality, relationships and self-improvement, that will help you manifest miracles in your life.

Staying on the Path
This book is an outstanding collection of Wayne's observations, created for those of you who are already on a spiritual path, as well as those of you who are just trying to get there. Full of wit and wisdom, *Staying on The Path* provides direction to keep you moving forward.

What Do You Really Want for Your Children
Wayne shares his ideas on how to raise happy, confident, well balanced children, with an appreciation for themselves and their place on this planet.

Your Erroneous Zones
Over 20 years since it was first published, this number one best-seller remains one of the most popular and practical self-actualisation books available today. Wayne's message is simple and direct: you can take control of who and what you are.

Your Sacred Self
In this extraordinary book, Wayne discusses your Sacred or Higher Self and helps you to understand the light that radiates within you. Wayne looks at the ways you can master the keys to higher awareness to make an impact on your life and others.

Have in your mind that which could constitute a miracle for you. Get the vision. Suspend disbelief and scepticism. Allow yourself to take the journey towards real magic.

Manifest Your Destiny
You have the power within you to attract to yourself all you could ever want. Understand your divine power and *Manifest Your Destiny*, using Wayne's amazing nine spiritual principles.

A Promise Is A Promise
Wayne and his wife, Marcelene, reveal their storytelling talent in their account of an almost unbelievable story. For the past 26 years, Edwarda O'Bara has been in a comatose state, and her mother has kept her promise to never leave her beloved daughter. This touching tale has much to teach about life and love.

Other titles of interest published by Rider . . .

AGELESS BODY, TIMELESS MIND
A Practical Alternative to Growing Old

Deepak Chopra

'Aging is much more of a choice than people ever dream.'

Few people are better qualified than Dr Deepak Chopra to show us the extent to which the reshaping of the aging process is within our control. A world-class pioneer in mind/body medicine, and an acclaimed exponent of the significance of the ancient Hindu teachings on Ayurveda, he is justly famous for explaining how our attitude towards ourselves can change the way we age. Interestingly, this exciting and revolutionary area of research is also being underpinned by contemporary discoveries in quantum physics.

Ageless Body, Timeless Mind has been a huge best-seller round the world. It combines lucid theory, case studies and a wealth of practical exercises to demonstrate the innate intelligence of the mind/body processes and the extent to which sickness and aging are created by nothing more than gaps in our self-knowledge. By increasing this self-knowledge, we can master simple yet effective ways to metabolize time, and so achieve our unbounded potential.

THE PATH TO LOVE
Spiritual Lessons for Creating the Love You Need

Deepak Chopra

In this groundbreaking and helpful book, influential teacher and physician, Deepak Chopra, explores how our hearts have lost their centre and why love so often falls short of filling a deep, aching need within us.

He also explains how we can rediscover the love we long for, one which is rich and meaningful, satisfying and lasting – by restoring to love its missing element: spirituality.

In presenting the long-forgotten, timeless laws of love, together with practical suggestions for bringing them to fruition, Deepak Chopra shows us how to transform our lives for ever – and the lives of those whom we love.

JOURNEY INTO HEALING
Awakening the Wisdom Within You

Deepak Chopra

In this volume, essential ideas from the work of Deepak Chopra are arranged to create a transcendent experience for the reader, a journey into healing. Along the path, we discover that what we think and feel can actually change our biology. We learn to go beyond self-imposed limitations that create disease, and to seek that place inside ourselves that is at one with the infinite intelligence of the universe, the source of life. By the end of this book, the reader's consciousness will have been altered by the experience of the journey itself. Such change has the power to transform our lives, to grace us with the gifts of lasting peace and perfect health.

The final pages contain techniques for the Mindfulness Meditation, which can access the silent space between your thoughts and tap into the inner wisdom that will make all your dreams come true.

THE WAY OF THE WIZARD
20 Spiritual Lessons for Creating the Life You Want

Deepak Chopra

In *The Way of the Wizard*, Deepak Chopra explains twenty life-enhancing principles for creating the life we want. Complete freedom and fulfilment come from rediscovering the magic we have lost – but that remains within our grasp. Once we have found the wizard, the inner guide, deep inside ourselves we will be lifted from the ordinary, humdrum world to a new one dominated by miracles.

This extraordinarily powerful book offers a series of lessons, together with full explanations and advice, on how to walk the wizard's way. The result is a practical and accessible guide to one of life's shortest but most rewarding journeys: the one into the realm of boundless possibilities that exists within and all around us.

FEEL THE FEAR . . . AND BEYOND
Dynamic Techniques for *Doing It Anyway*

Susan Jeffers

'To read this book is eye-opening; to USE this book is life-changing.'

Internationally renowned author, Susan Jeffers, has helped millions of people round the globe to overcome their fears and heal the pain in their lives. Her now classic work, *Feel The Fear And Do It Anyway*, has been a huge worldwide success and continues to ride high in the bestseller charts because it showed us all, in simple terms, how to transform our anxieties into confidence, action and love.

Feel The Fear . . . And Beyond is the long-awaited companion to this important book – yet it also stands alone as a must-have for facing life at the end of the twentieth century . . . and beyond. Filled with valuable exercises, it is designed to teach us that we can handle whatever life brings us in a powerful and life-affirming way. Susan Jeffers encourages us to make full use of these valuable tools when we are fearful of making changes or confronting new situations in our lives.

For individual and group use – including tips for use with children – as well as your own '30 Day Power Planner'.

This inspiring and empowering book will bring welcome relief to anyone who is ever worried or afraid.

DESCENDANTS
Tracking the Past . . . Healing the Future

Denise Linn

'Bold and visionary methods that create a powerful blueprint for a positive future' *Deepak Chopra*

'In our every deliberation, we must consider the impact of our decisions on the next seven generations' *From the Great Law of the American Indian Iroquois Confederacy*

We are shaped by our past. The way we perceive the world is a direct result of the influence of our immediate family, our ancestors and our cultural roots.

In this inspirational yet down-to-earth book, lecturer and healer Denise Linn shows us how to draw upon the wellspring of ancestral wisdom that dwells within us. She also suggests how to identify and heal the negative aspects of this inheritance, to avoid passing the mistakes of the past onto those who come after us.

Descendants offers a remarkable blueprint for the times ahead. By following the many practical ideas within, we can create a legacy of hope, love and joy to be handed down through the generations – and into the future.

If you would like to order any of the following or to receive our catalogue please fill in the form below:

Ageless Body, Timeless Mind by Deepak Chopra	£7.99
The Path to Love by Deepak Chopra	£9.99
Journey Into Healing by Deepak Chopra	£8.99
The Way of the Wizard by Deepak Chopra	£9.99
Feel the Fear . . . And Beyond by Susan Jeffers	£8.99
Descendants by Denise Linn	£9.99

HOW TO ORDER

BY POST: TBS Direct, TBS Ltd, Colchester Road, Frating Green, Essex CO7 7DW

Please send me _____ copies of   @ £   each

☐ I enclose my cheque for £ _____ payable to Rider Books

☐ Please charge £ _____ to my American Express/Visa/Mastercard account*
  (*delete as applicable)

Card No ☐☐☐☐☐☐☐☐☐☐☐☐☐☐☐☐☐☐☐☐

Expiry Date: ☐☐☐☐   Signature _____

Name _____

Address _____

_____ Postcode _____

Delivery address if different _____

_____ Postcode _____

Or call our credit card hotline on 01206 255800.
Please have your card details handy.

Please quote reference: WD

Rider is an imprint of Random House UK Ltd

Please tick here if you do not wish to receive further information from Rider or associated companies ☐